COMPLETE THE RHYME

Choose any one of the objects below to complete the
following rhyme:

Jeff and Megan went to
the playground
And found a penny,
shiny and_____!

BOWL

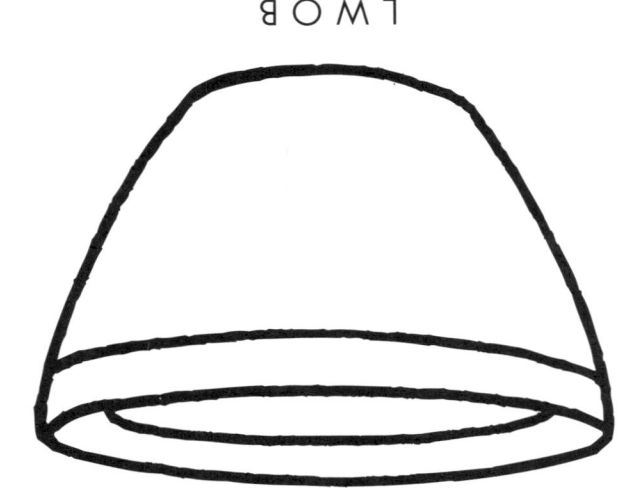

FIRYNGPNA

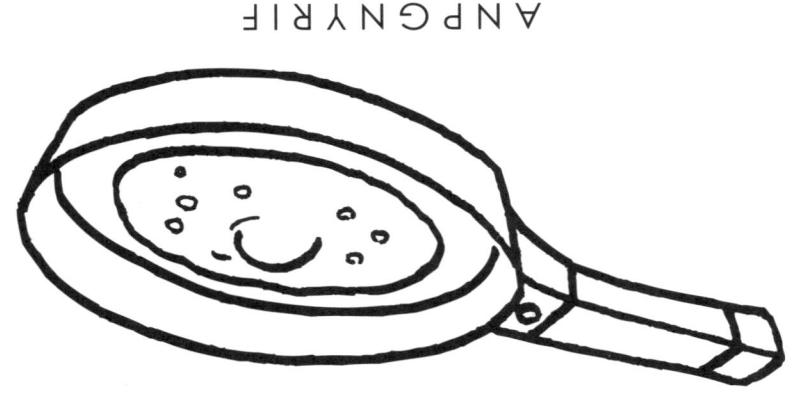

JUMBLED WORDS ON PICTURES

WHAT AM I?

You can hear me and see me too
I can tell what's happening all around you
News, cartoons, movies, and songs
Now can you guess, what am I?

COMPLETE THE RHYME

Choose any one of the objects below to complete the following rhyme:

Sally and Tom went to the
toy shop
Tom chose a car and Sally,
a toy_____!

JUMBLED WORDS ON PICTURES

L B T E A

L V O S H E

WHAT COLOR AM I?

I am the color of the sky
And I paint the sea too
Sometimes you find me in beach balls and umbrellas
Can you tell me what color am I?

COMPLETE THE RHYME

Choose any one of the objects below to complete the
following rhyme:

The garden has _____ red,
white, and blue
And pink, purple, and yellow
too!

Candy

Car

Flowers

WHAT SHAPE AM I?

I am a shape that you see everyday
In icecream cones, pizzas, and pyramids too
Your math teacher draws me
Hey kids, can you name me?

PICTURE CROSSWORD

Write the names of the objects in the boxes next to their pictures, and find out what keeps your feet dry in winter.

FINDING SHAPES

Can you find these shapes in the picture below?
Color the ones you find.

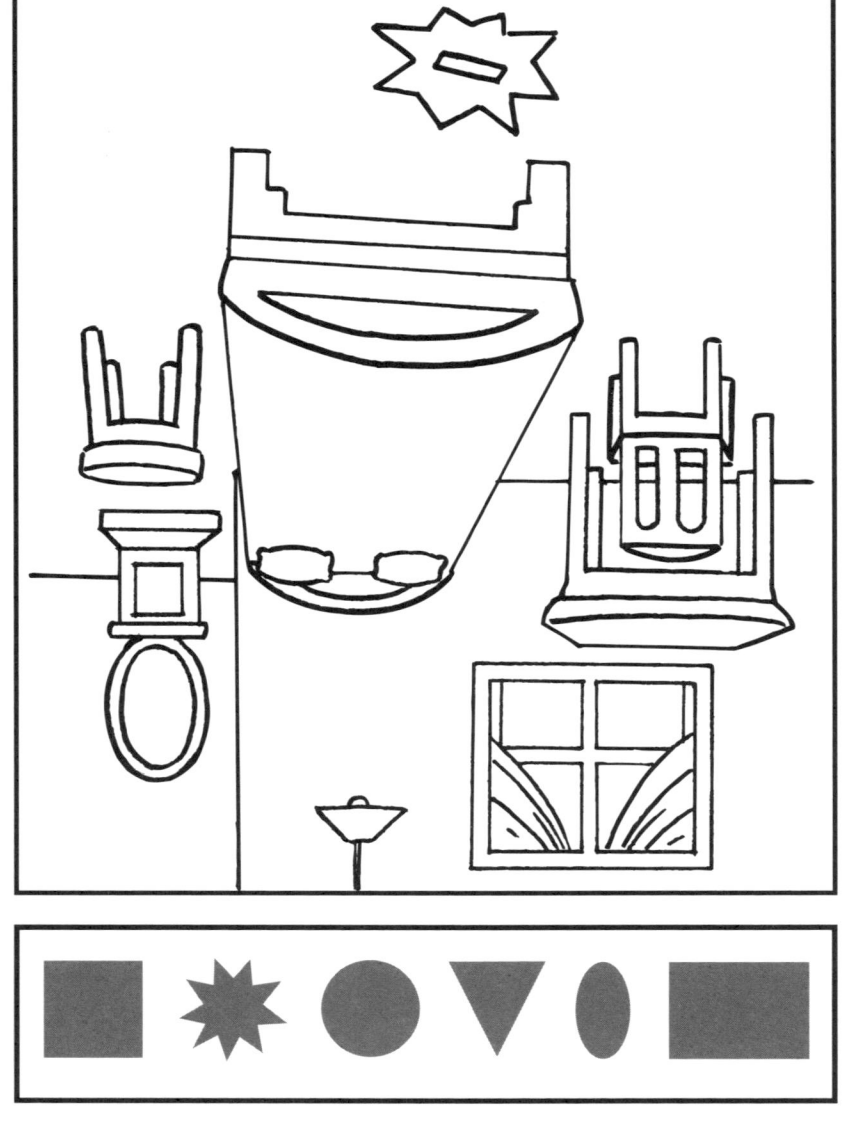

PICTURE CROSSWORD

Fill in the boxes below the objects to find out what you use to write to people with.

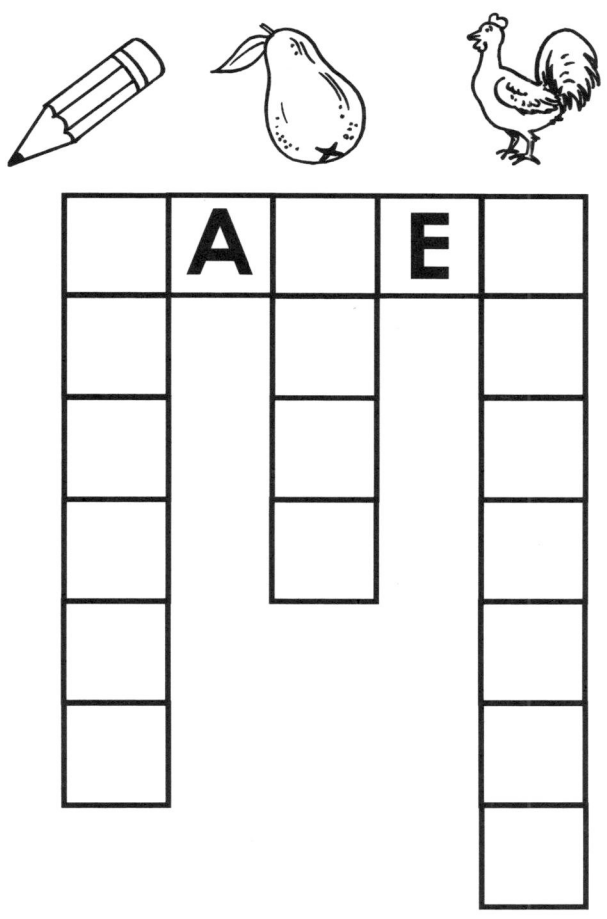

	A		E	

WHAT BELONGS?

Jane is going on a picnic. Help her pack by picking the objects she will need:

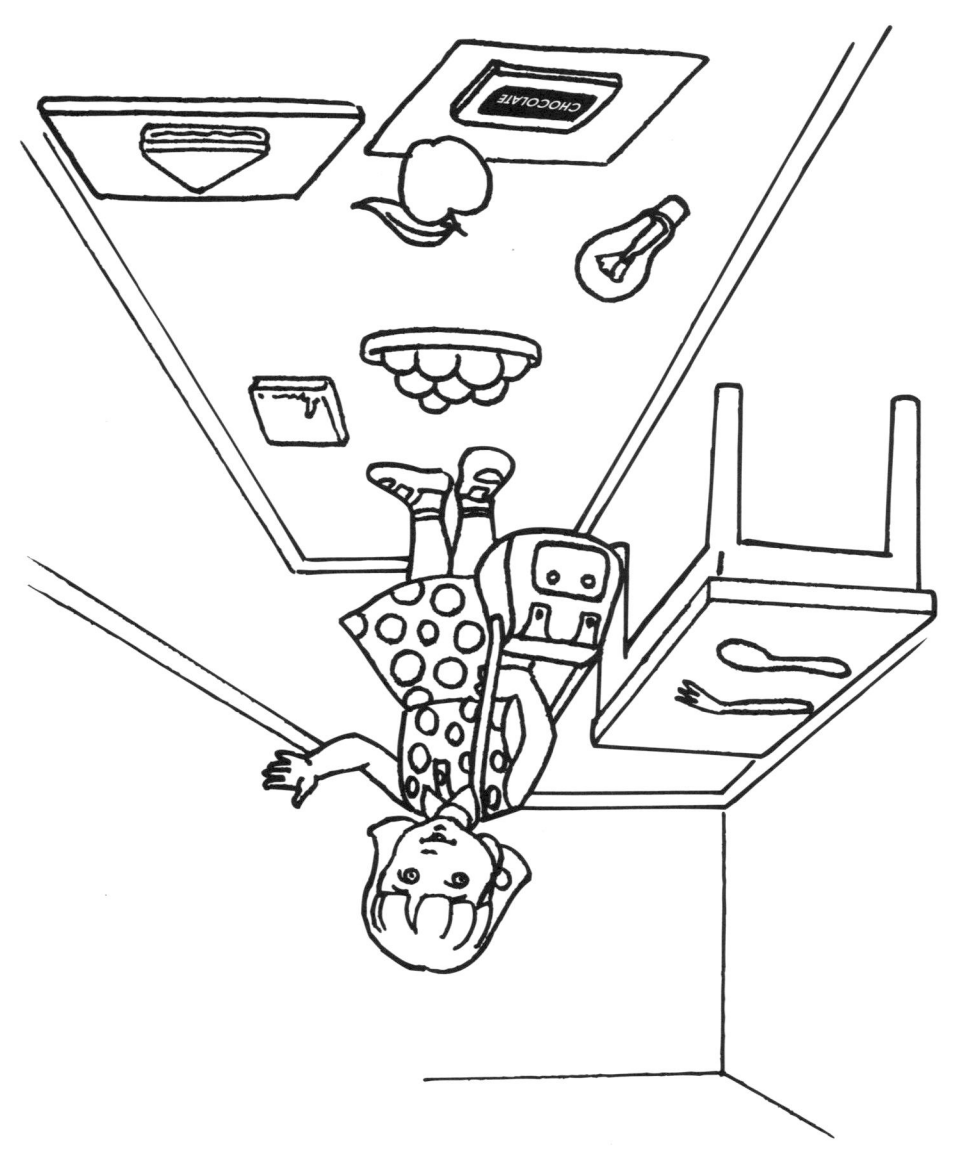

FINDING SHAPES

Can you find these shapes in the picture below?
Color the ones you find.

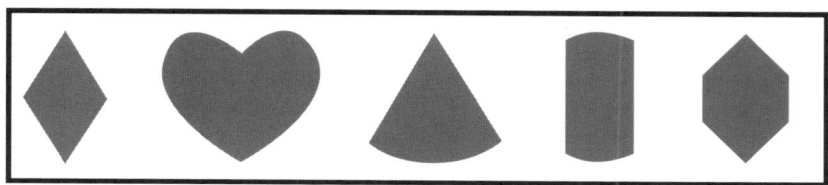

PICTURE CROSSWORD

Write the names of the objects in the boxes next to their pictures, and find out what you need at the beach.

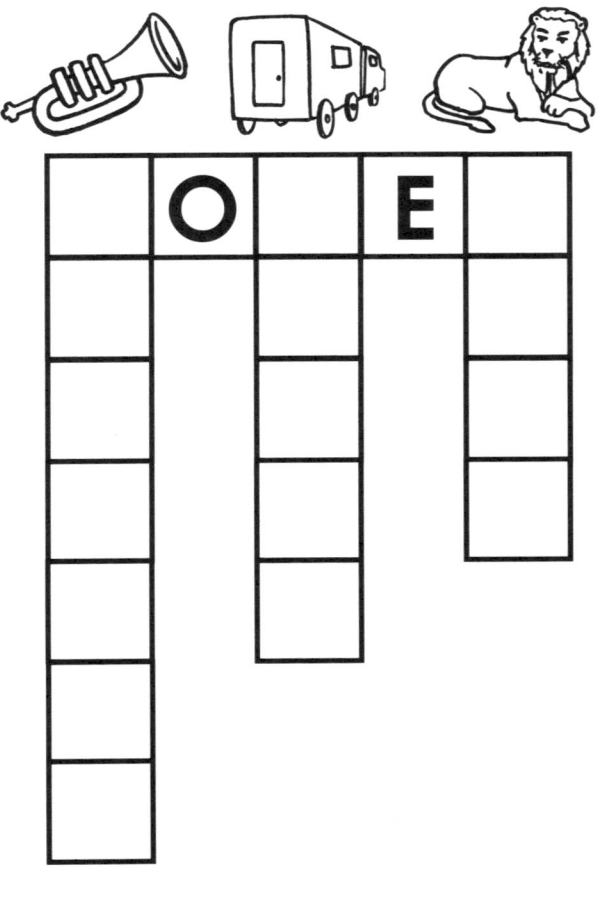

WHAT BELONGS?

John is getting ready for school. Pick the things that he needs to take with him.

WORD ASSOCIATION

Where is Joanna planning to go with her friends this Sunday? Find out by using the first letter of each object you see below:

WORD BLOCKS

Jenny loves to help her mom do this when she is free!
Find out what it is by using the first letter of each object
below:

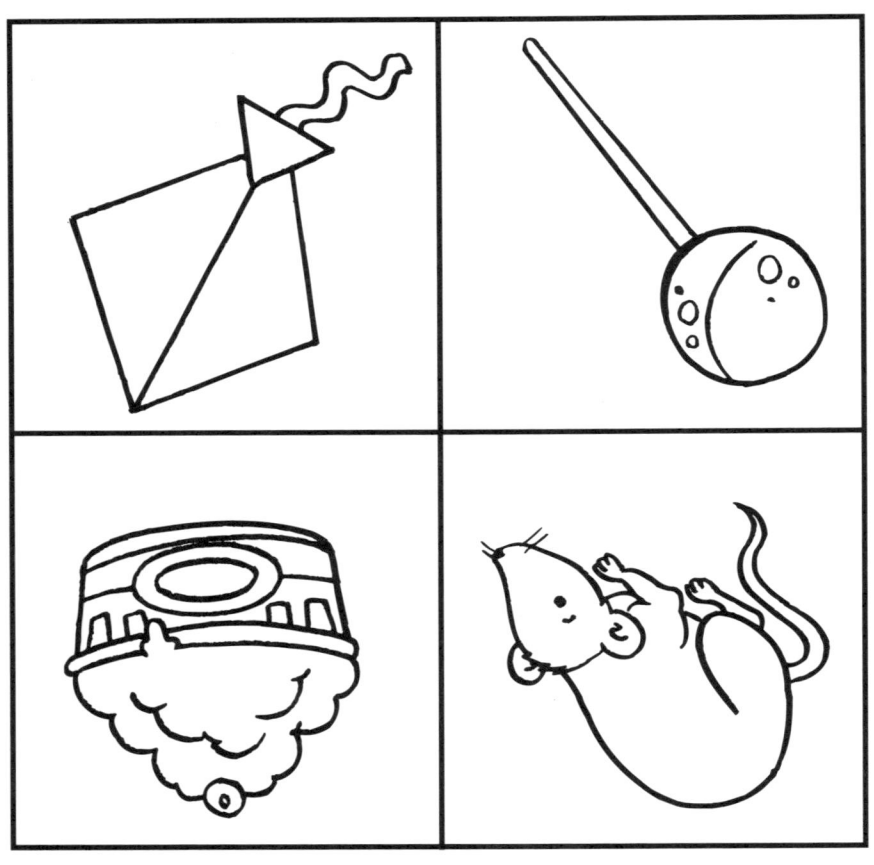

WORD BLOCKS

Jack does not like to drink this at breakfast. Find out what it is by using the first letter of each object that you see below:

CONNECT THE DOTS

Connect the dots to find out a popular object that you see in a playground.

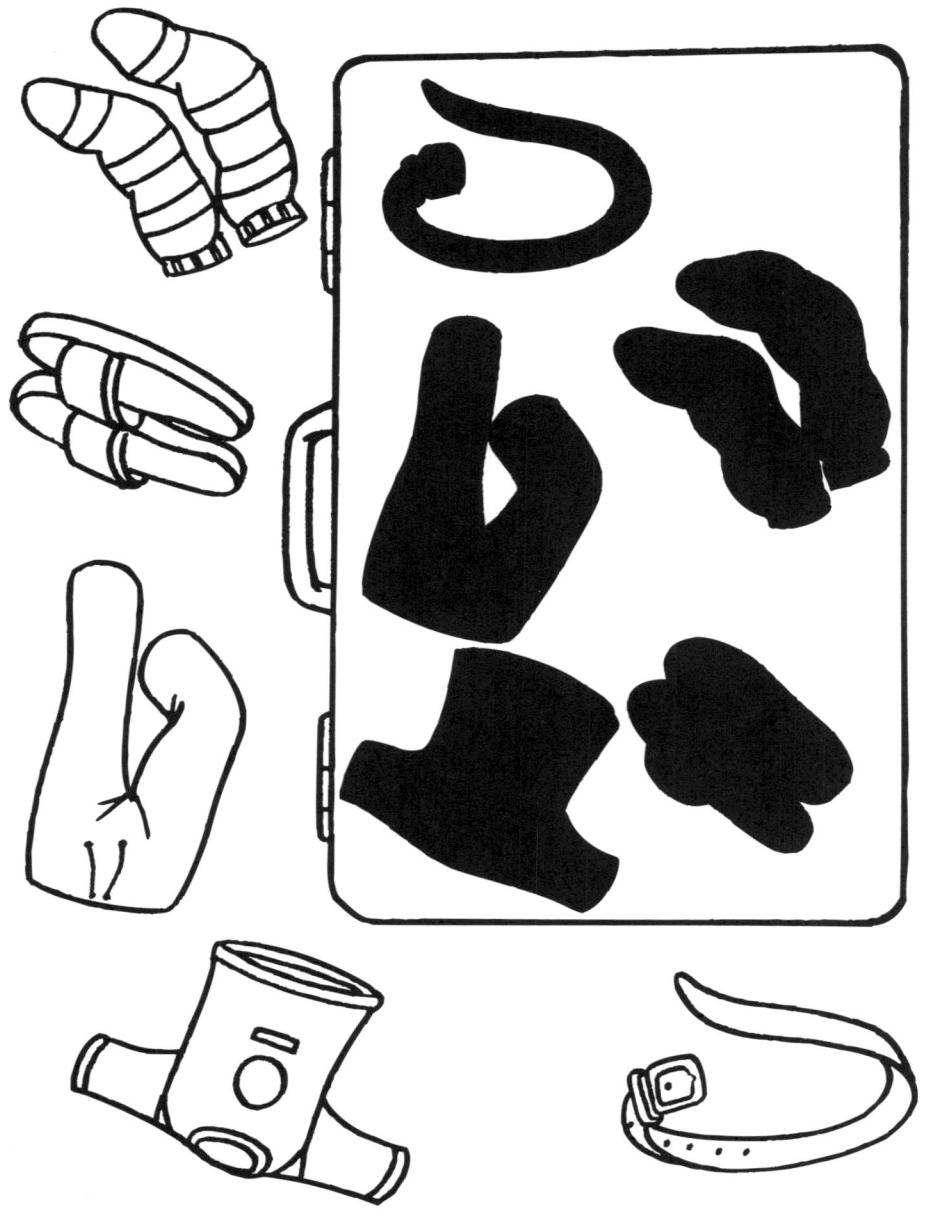

SHADOW MATCHING

Match the objects to their shadows inside the suitcase:

CONNECT THE DOTS

Connect the dots and find out what mom loves to do.

COMPLETE THE PICTURE

NOT LIKE THE OTHERS

Which one of the following objects cannot
be found at a gas station?

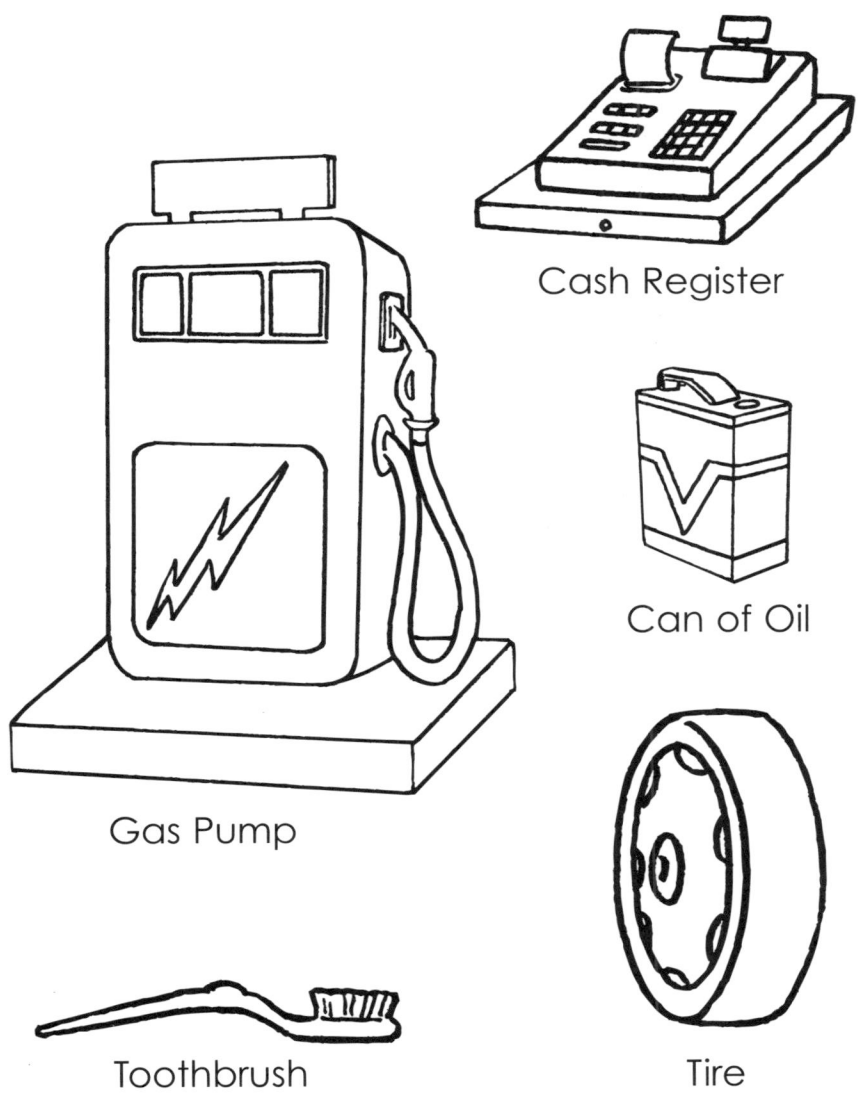

Cash Register

Can of Oil

Gas Pump

Toothbrush

Tire

NOT LIKE THE OTHERS

Find the object that is not like the others in the group:

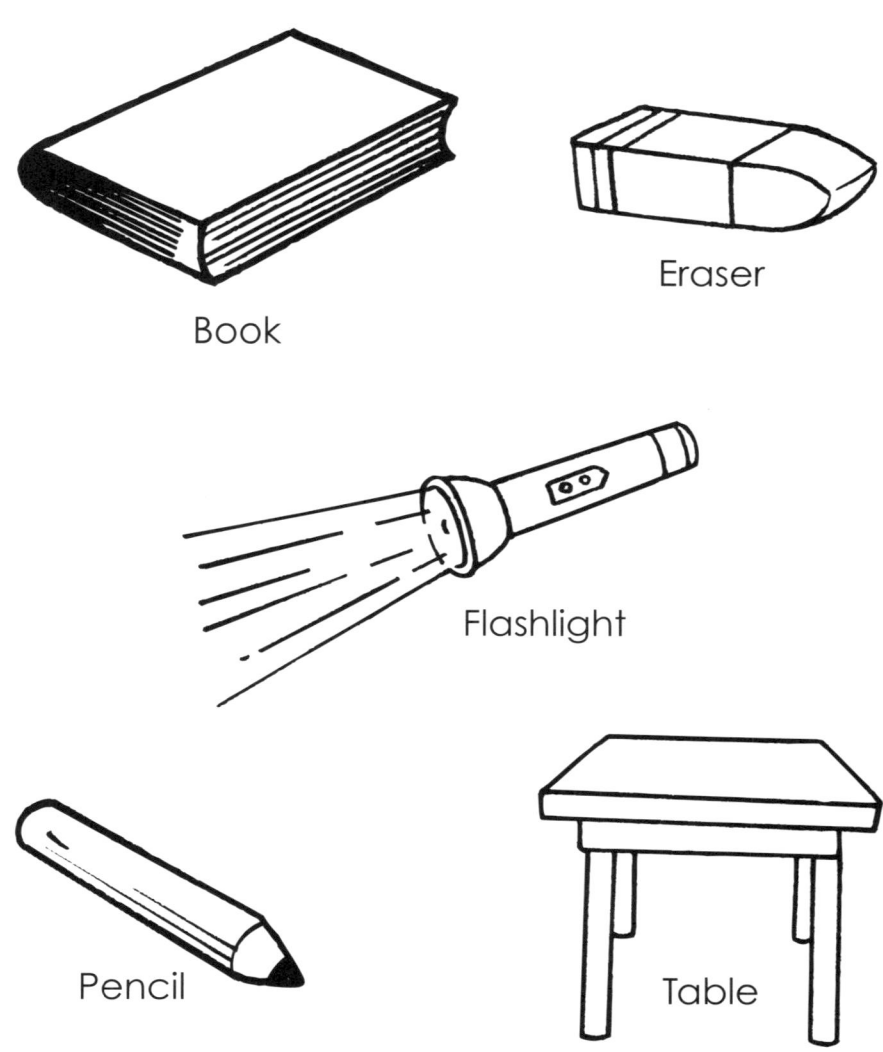

Book

Eraser

Flashlight

Pencil

Table

SHADOW MATCHING

Match the objects to their shadows in the picnic basket:

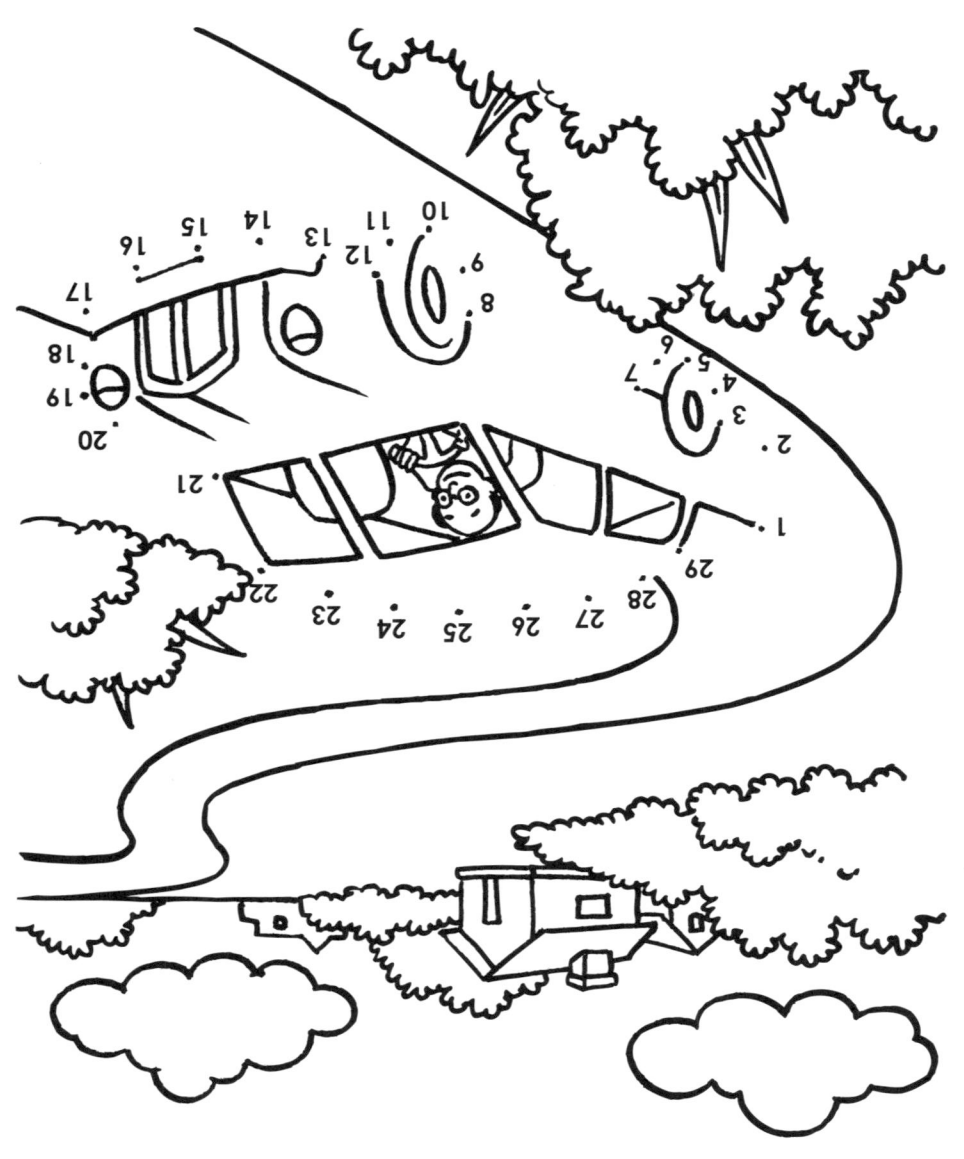

CONNECT THE DOTS

Connect the dots to help dad travel to work!

COLOR BY NUMBERS

Fill out the numbers in the given colors to see how some children get to school.

Color Chart: 1-Sky Blue, 2-Orange, 3-Dark Green, 4-Yellow, 5-Light Green, 6-Dark Blue, 7-Red, 8-Black, 9-Brown

NOT LIKE THE OTHERS

Karen went to Paris this summer. Guess what she did NOT see at the airport:

Flight Attendant

Plane

Rowboat

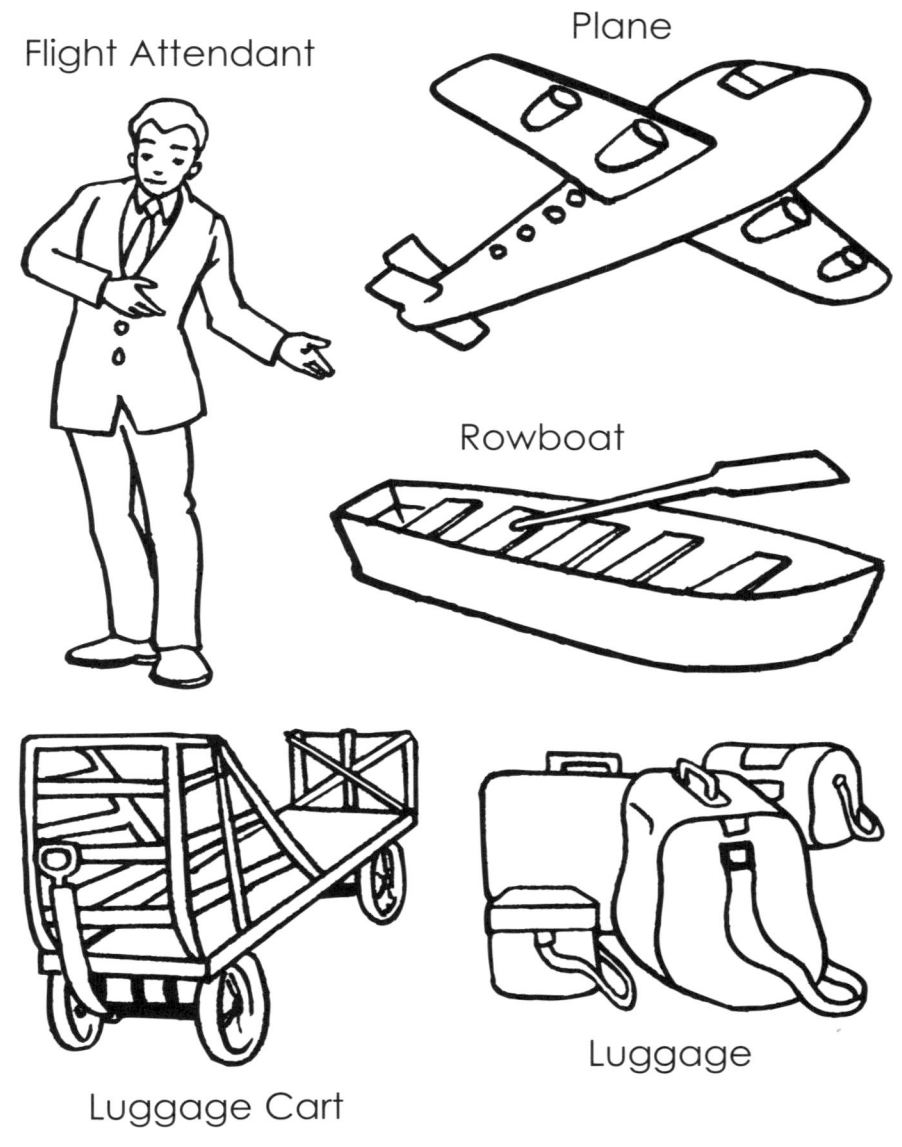

Luggage Cart

Luggage

CONNECT THE DOTS

Where do Pat and her friends hold their secret club meetings? Connect the dots to find out.

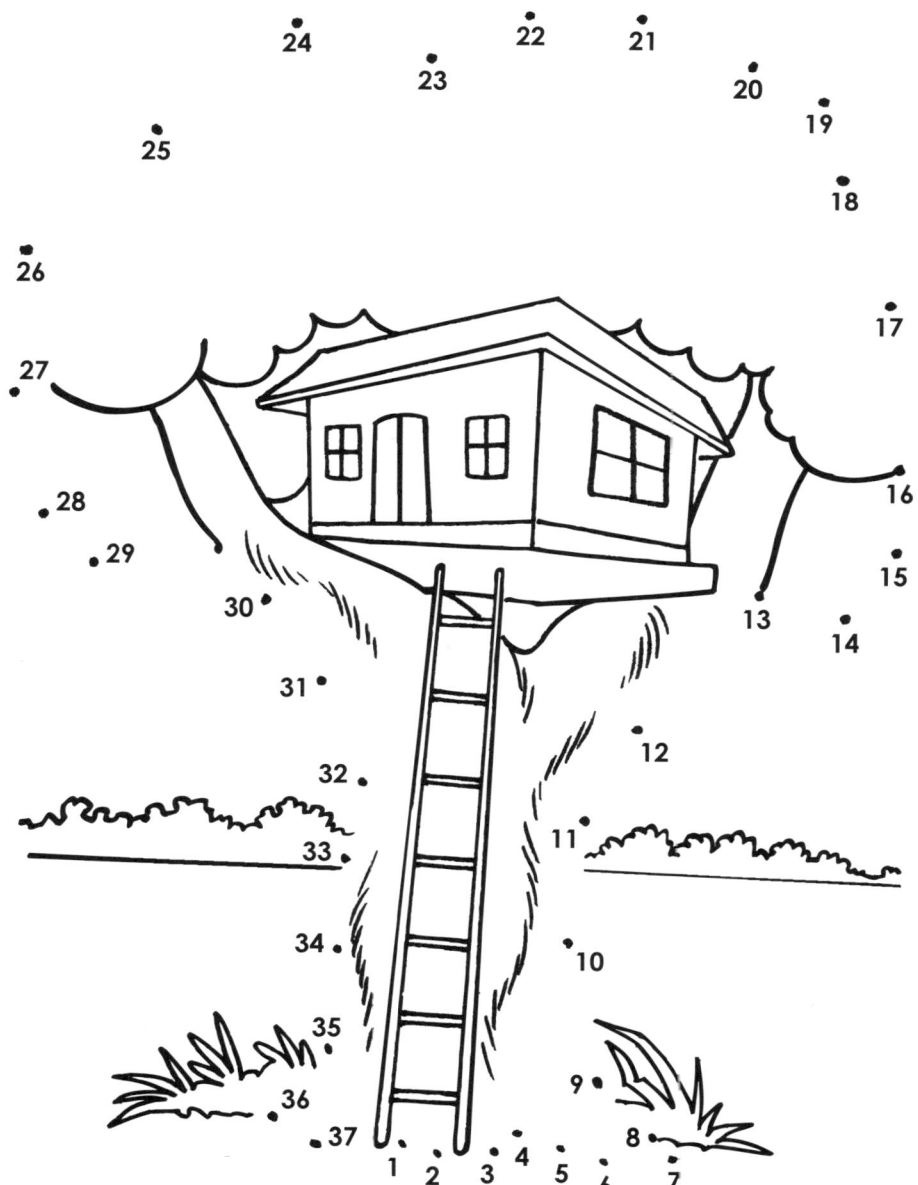

Color Chart: 1-Orange, 2-Light Blue, 3-Black, 4-Brown,
5-Red, 6-Pink, 7-Purple, 8-Dark Blue, 9-Green

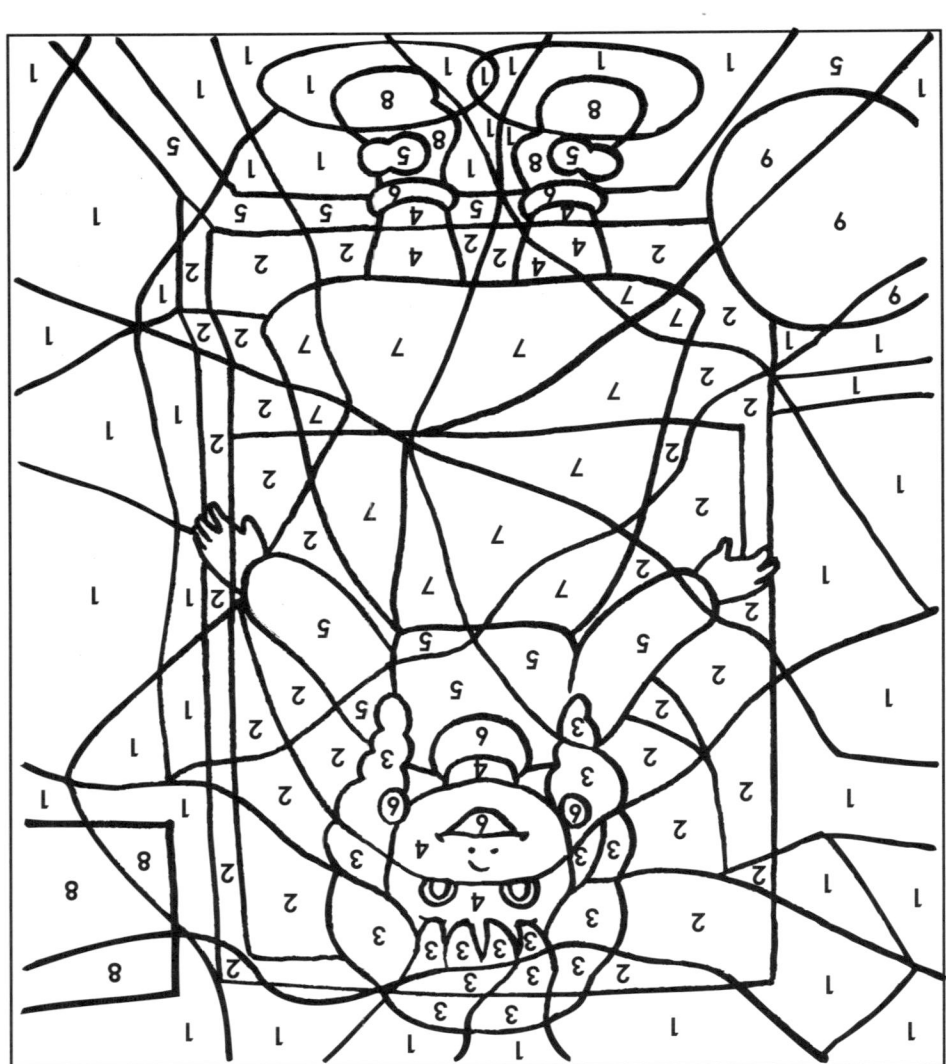

Find out who lives in Betty's playroom by filling in the
numbers according to the color chart:

COLOR BY NUMBERS

GRID DRAWING

Copy the drawing in the empty grid given below.

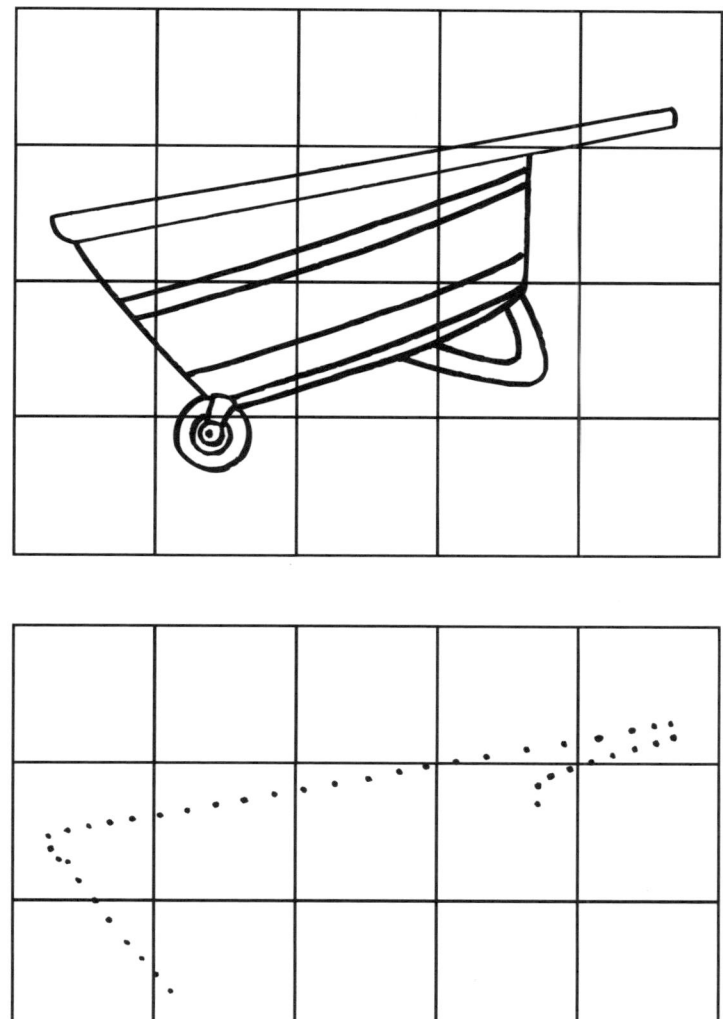

CONNECT THE DOTS

Connect the dots to find out what the Williams family is doing this weekend.

COMPLETE THE PICTURE

GRID DRAWING

Copy the complete drawing in the empty
grid given below.

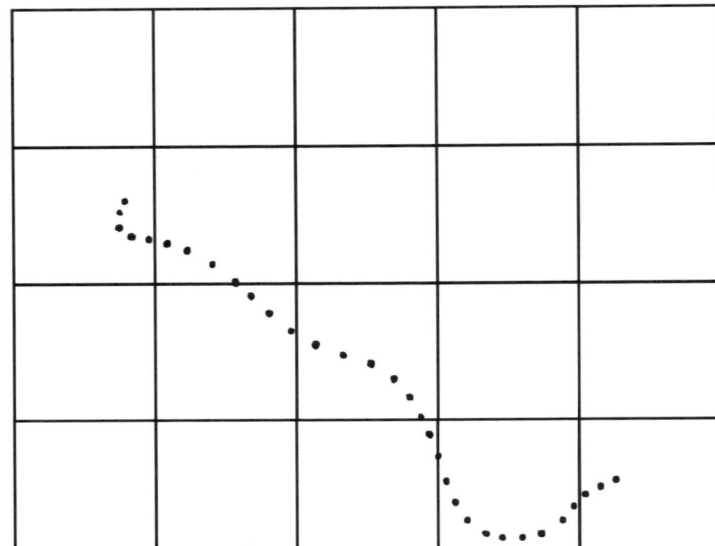

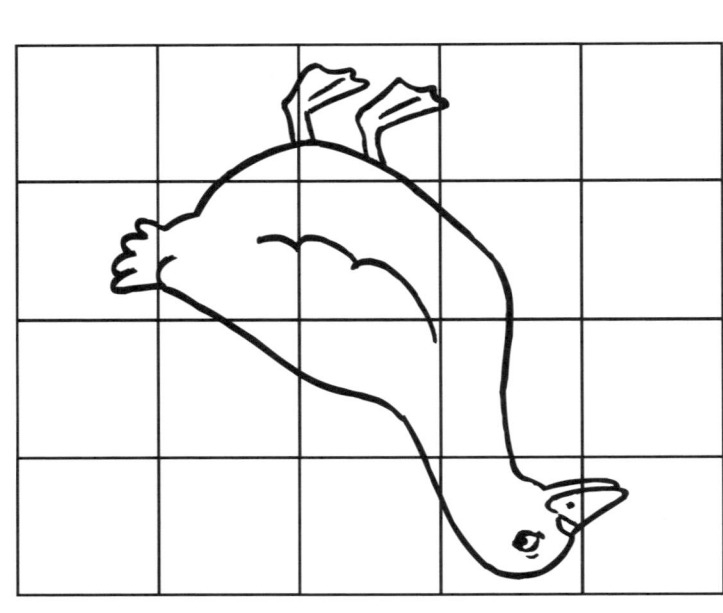

COLOR BY NUMBERS

What are the kids at the playground waiting for? Color by the numbers and find out!

Color Chart: 1-Blue, 2-Yellow, 3-Orange, 4-Black,
5-Purple, 6-Red, 7-Green, 8-Brown

Answer : 1. The bottom tray has no peas; 2. The bottom tray has a spoon instead of a kinfe; 3. The bottom tray has honey instead of butter; 4. The bread on the bottom tray is not sliced, 5. Instead of an apple, the bottom tray has an orange.

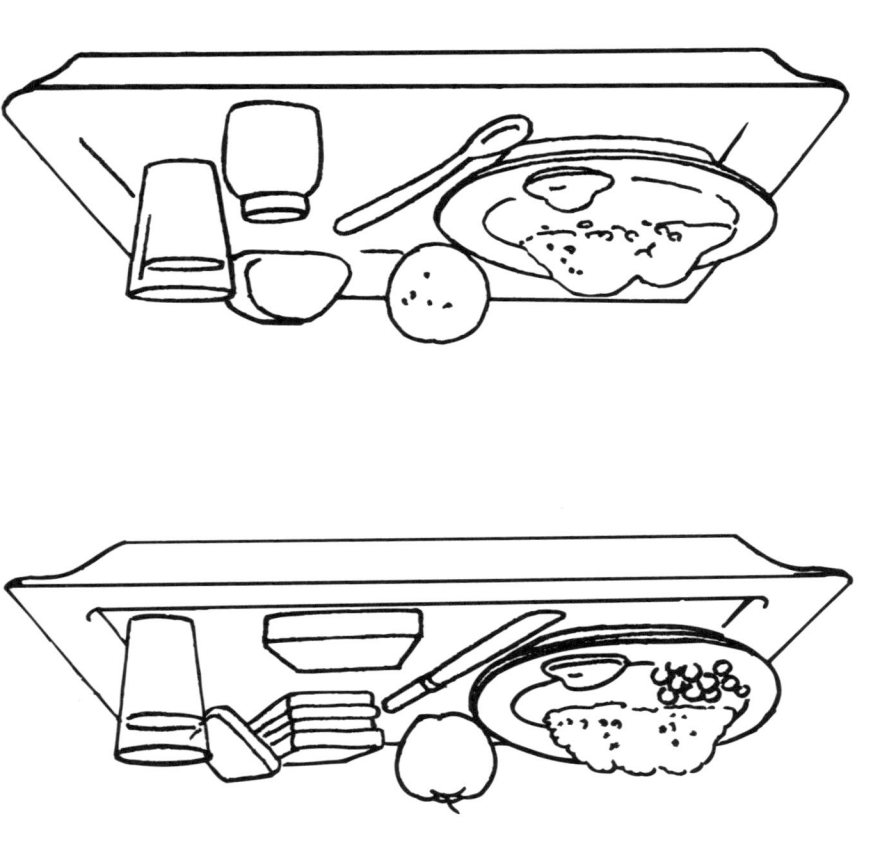

Find 5 differences between the pictures below.

FIND THE DIFFERENCE

COUNTING BY PICTURES

Circle the number of objects given below:

Circle: 1 2 3 4 5

Circle: 1 2 3 4 5

Circle: 1 2 3 4 5

Circle: 1 2 3 4 5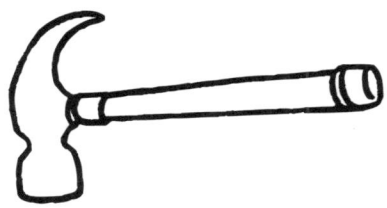

COUNTING BY PICTURES

How many animals do you see in the pictures below? Circle the number below each picture:

Circle: 1 2 3 4 5

Circle: 1 2 3 4 5

Circle: 1 2 3 4 5

Circle: 1 2 3 4 5

FIND THE DIFFERENCE

Can you find 5 differences between the two pictures?

Meg

Laura

Answer: 1. Meg is wearing a polka-dotted dress, while Laura is wearing a plain dress; 2. Laura is not wearing a hat; 3. Laura's dress has no pockets; 4. Laura's shoes have no buckels; 5. Laura has no buttons on her dress.

GRID DRAWING

Copy the drawing in the empty grid given below.

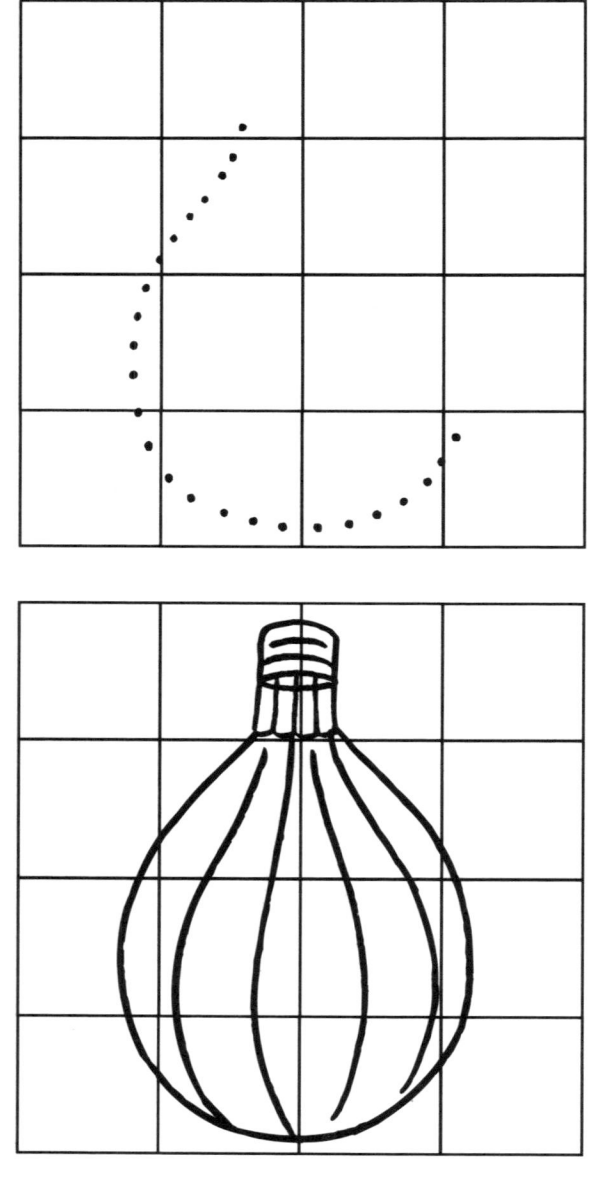

COLOR BY NUMBERS

Find out Danny's favorite pet by striking out all the letters that appear twice in the grid:

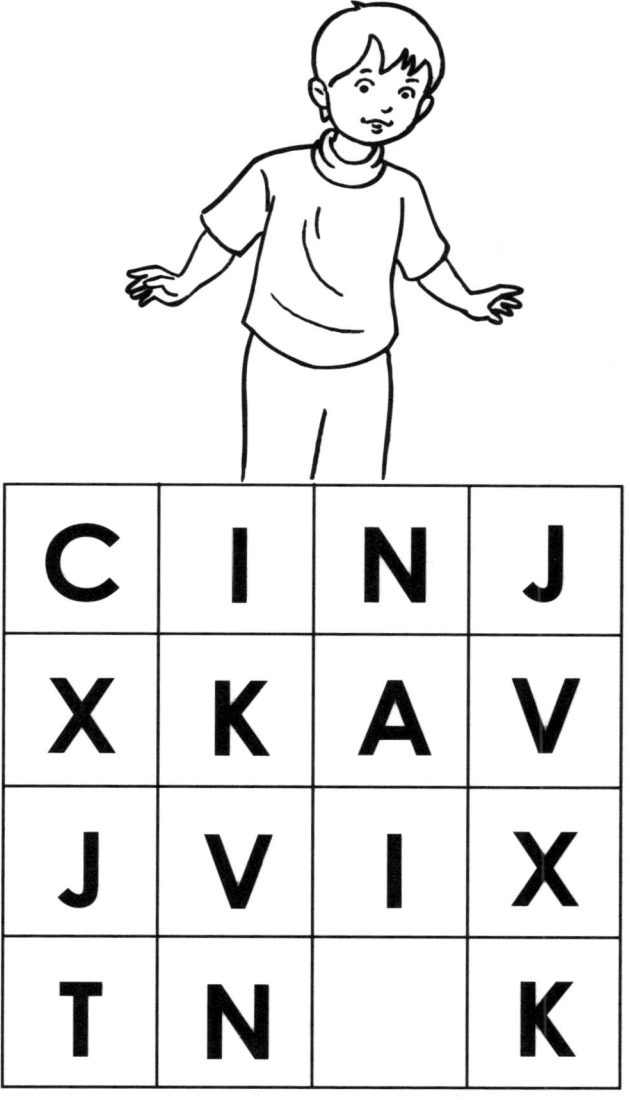

C	I	N	J
X	K	A	V
J	V	I	X
T	N		K

Answer:1. Picture 1 has three bottles, while Picture 2 has only two; 2. In Picture 2, there are only three drawer knobs; 3.The brush in Picture 2 has no hadnle; 4. In Picture 2' there is no pearl necklace.

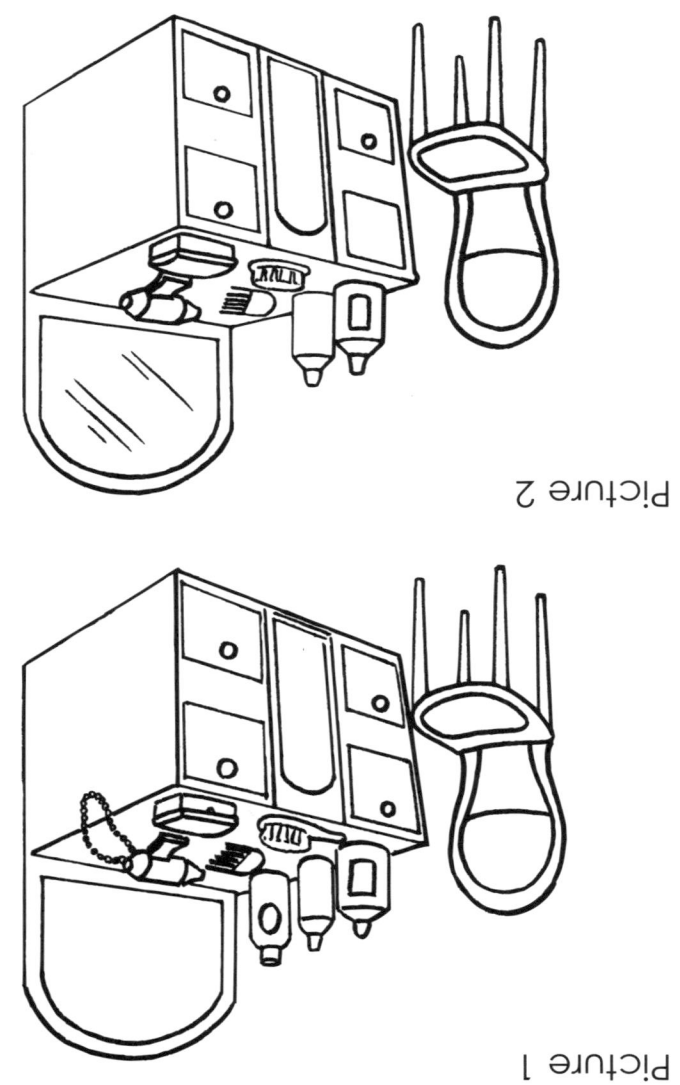

Picture 2

Picture 1

Circle the 4 differences between the two pictures:

FIND THE DIFFERENCE

COMPLETE THE STORY

Fill in the blanks with the help of the pictures and word clues and complete the story:

Word Clues: *Letter, cookies, package, bike, car, chocolate, oatmeal*

Mother told Peter to go to the mailbox and mail

a _____  . On the way, Peter saw

his friend Jack on

his_____ . Jack was going to the

candy

store to buy some_____ . Peter's

mouth watered and he hurried off to complete his

job! After mailing the letter in the mailbox,

Peter joined Jack, and the two friends went off to

the candy store and had their fill!

MATCH THE PICTURES

Match the objects in both the columns:

Socks

Eraser

Fork

Paintbrush

Pencil

Shoes

Paint Bucket

Knife

CROSS-OUT PUZZLES

Cross out all the letters appearing 5 times to find out which ride at the amusement park Maggie likes the most:

A	Z	Y	D	W	B	Y
R	Q	E	Q	W	L	L
D	B	Q	Z	Y	F	Z
Z	F	F	B	D	O	E
T	E	R	Y	W	R	C
■	Z	Q	W	B	Q	D
A	S	B	D	Y	E	W

CROSS-OUT PUZZLES

What did Alex do at the beach? Cross out all the letters appearing 3 times in the grid below to spell out the answer:

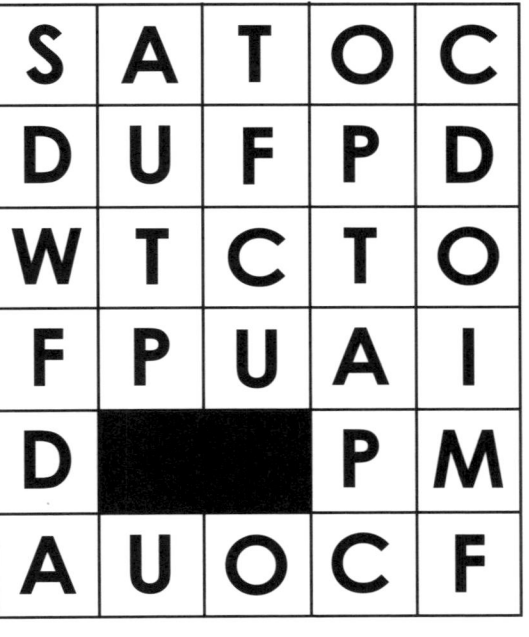

S	A	T	O	C
D	U	F	P	D
W	T	C	T	O
F	P	U	A	I
D	▮	▮	P	M
A	U	O	C	F

FIND THE DIFFERENCE

Circle what is missing in the pictures below:

COMPLETE THE STORY

Fill in the blanks with the help of the picture and word clues given to complete the story:

Word Clues: *Flute, Recorder, Guitar, Piano, Saxophone, Cello, Violin*

Pam loved music classes at

school. Her favorite instrument

was the _____.

But she also liked to strum

on the _____.

Her friend Elizabeth, however, liked

to sing. Pam and Elizabeth did not

like the sound of the_____.

They thought it was too sad.

MATCH THE PICTURES

Match the opposites by pairing up the pictures below:

Fat

White

Hot

Slow

Black

Thin

Fast

Girl

Boy

Cold

Answers: Boy & Girl, Hot & Cold, Fast & Slow, Black & White, Fat & Thin

MAZE

Help Amy find her way to the bookstore
at the shopping mall.

MATCH THE PICTURES

Match the objects with the words:

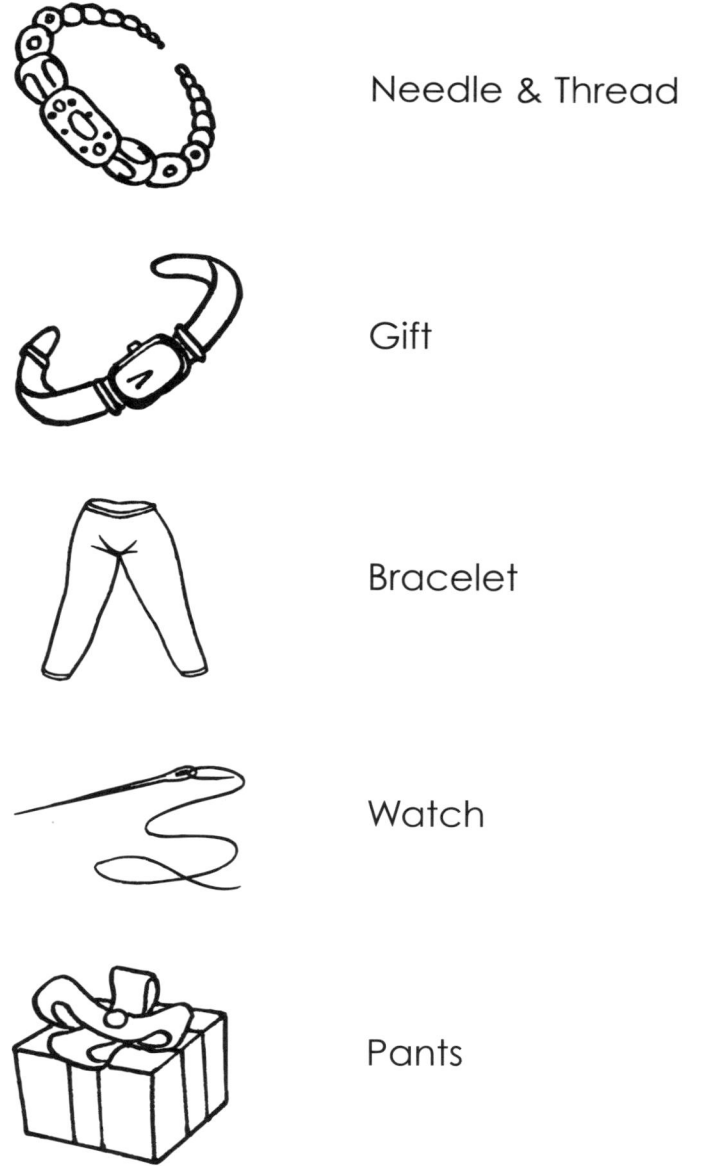

Needle & Thread

Gift

Bracelet

Watch

Pants

SCRAMBLED PICTURES

Can you count the number of rings given
in the picture below?

HIDDEN WORDS

Derek visited his dad's workplace. Can you find all the things he saw there?

D	X	S	T	K	Y	G	S
E	F	R	S	E	O	L	T
E	Z	E	E	Z	A	U	A
F	D	P	Z	S	N	E	P
F	W	A	O	C	P	Q	L
O	V	P	H	F	I	L	E
C	O	M	P	U	T	E	R

MATCH THE PICTURES

Pair up the pictures of hats by connecting them
with lines:

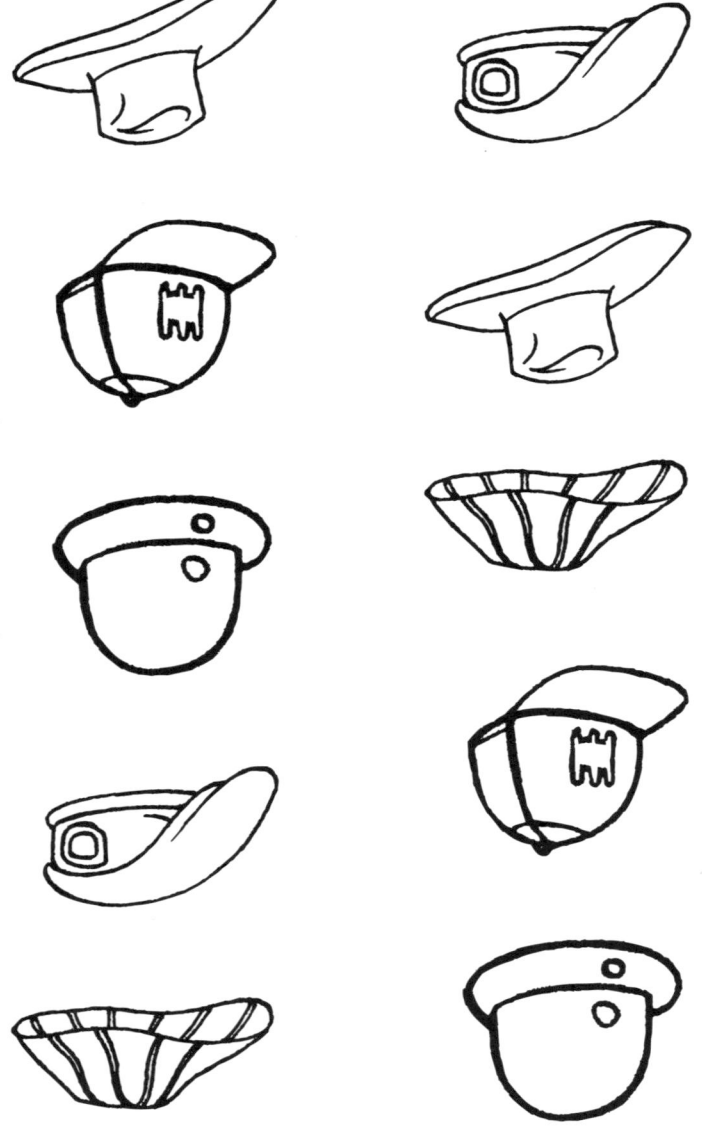

MAZE

Andy, Tanya, and Sam are going on a treasure hunt.
Who will get to the treasure chest?

MAZE

Can you help Morgan the Mouse reach his house before
Chad the Cat catches him?

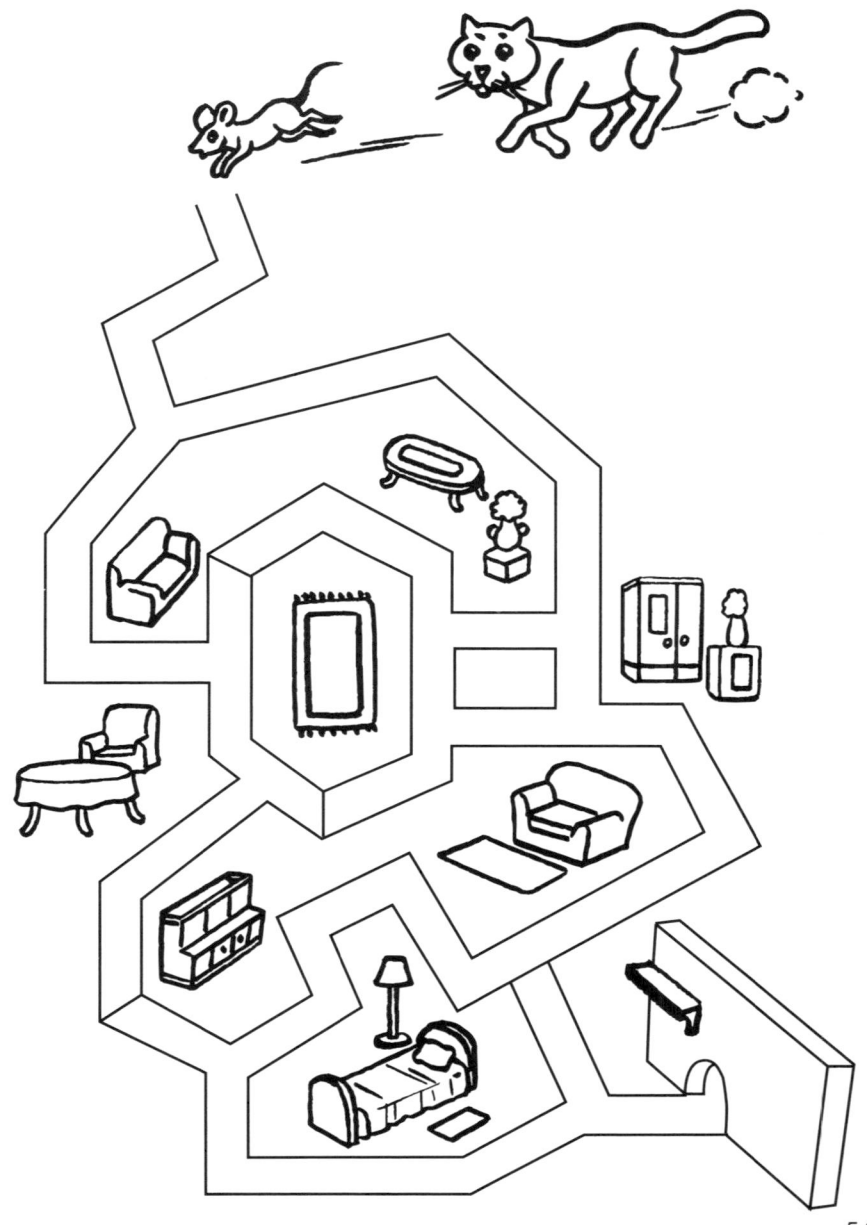

SCRAMBLED PICTURES

How many safety pins can you spot?

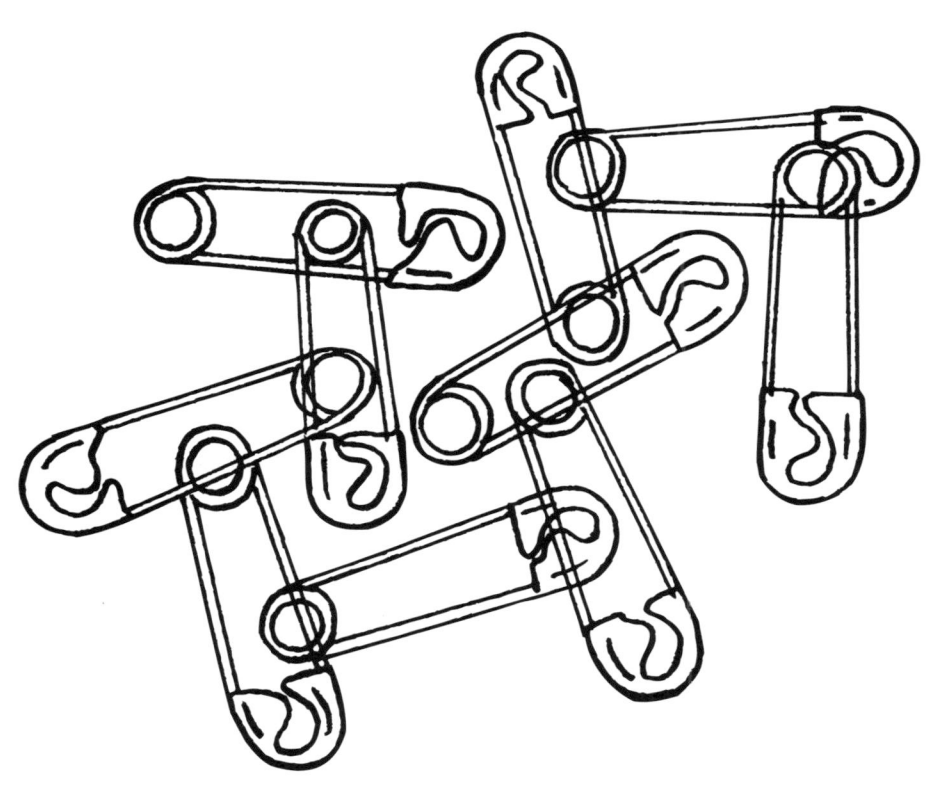

CROSSWORD

Use the clues given below to fill out the crossword puzzle with things that are found in a bathroom.

Across

1 You can stand under this to get clean

3 Something you look at yourself in

4 This is found on your sink and water flows out when you open it

5 You use this to dry yourself after a bath

Down

1 You clean your hair with this

2 You use this to clean your body and face

5 You can relax and soak in bubbles in the bath____.

HIDDEN WORDS

Rachel went to the supermarket with Aunt Sophie.
Find all the things they bought!

F	X	L	I	O	D	Y	E
R	I	Z	A	S	F	S	S
U	R	S	P	E	E	G	F
I	J	A	H	M	R	G	E
T	O	N	K	F	B	E	H
S	E	U	S	S	I	T	C

COLOR

Color the big buttons in green and
the small buttons in red

CROSSWORD

Mr. Stone took his history class to the museum for the day. What all did he show them? Find out by using the clues to fill out the word puzzle!

Across

1 Old vessels made of clay

3 Old money, the kinds that were made of gold or silver

4 Objects given to honor brave soldiers or winners of games

Down

1 Artwork that can be hung on the wall

2 Precious objects, especially those buried by pirates

3 Historical clothes

HIDDEN WORDS

What kind of animals did Fred and Pam find at the pet store?

A	T	O	P	C	K	G	F
I	S	R	A	B	B	I	T
E	L	T	R	U	T	Z	X
Y	W	Y	R	A	N	A	C
V	Q	D	O	G	P	M	J
M	R	E	T	S	M	A	H

Answer: Dog, Cat, Turtle, Canary, Hamster, Parrot, Rabbit

SPELL OUT

Look at the sets of pictures below and use them to name new objects:

_____

Use the first 2 letters of tree and the last 3 letters of duck to find out what carries our garbage away.

_____

Use the first 2 letters of plane & last 3 letters of skate to name something that we use at the dining table.

_____

Use the first 2 letters of book & last 2 letters of goat to name an object we use for traveling on water.

CROSSWORD

Fill out the word puzzle to find out what kinds of things Ronnie had fun with at the amusement park. Then unscramble the circled letters in the completed crossword to name a shape.

Across

1 This ride goes up and down and makes you scream out loud!

4 A pink and sticky candy that looks like Santa's beard

5 Get wet and have fun sliding down this

6 A fun race with cars!

Down

2 Go through this haunted place to get spooked!

3 Have a merry time going around and around on this one!

7 A ride in which you sit inside a kitchen vessel

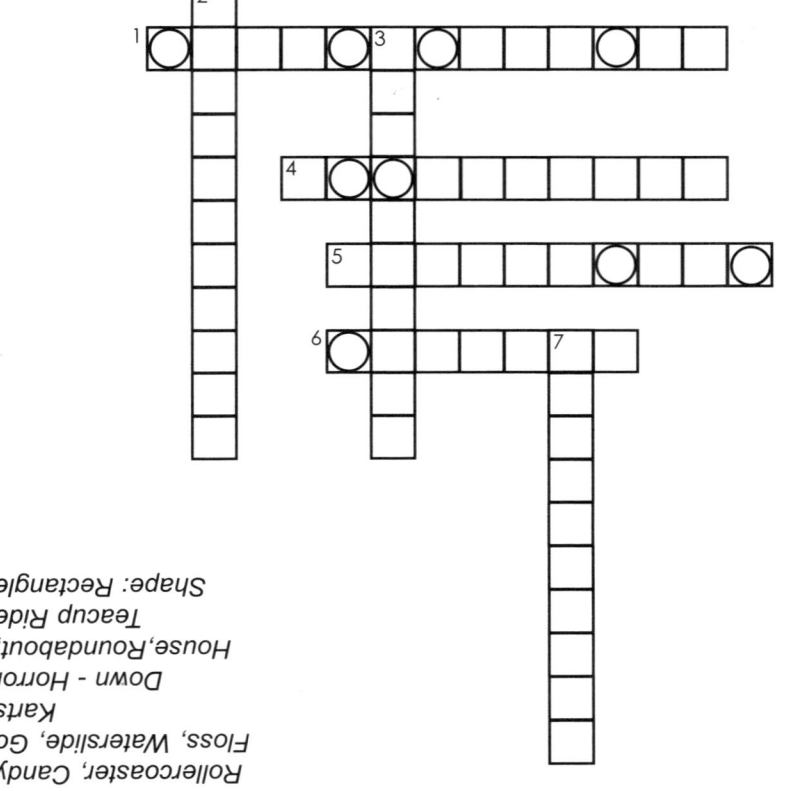